M000189576

Test Tube with a View

poems by

Shira Richman

Finishing Line Press
Georgetown, Kentucky

Test Tube with a View

ACKNOWLEDGMENTS

"Thank you to the editors of *The Pinch*, where "[please read silently]" first
appeared."

Publisher: Leah Maines

Editor: Christen Kincaid

Cover Art: Shira Richman

Author Photo: Tracy Goodsmith

Cover Design: Elizabeth Maines

Printed in the USA on acid-free paper.
Order online: www.finishinglinepress.com
also available on amazon.com

Author inquiries and mail orders:
Finishing Line Press
P. O. Box 1626
Georgetown, Kentucky 40324
U. S. A.

Table of Contents

I.

The bats do not need applause.
If you clap, they will change direction.
—Nuar Alsadir, "Bats"

[please read silently]

here it's so quiet the leaf
shushes you as it falls,
so quiet
quiet holds
its breath, has
nowhere to make
a call to the waiting, quiet
as the listening
and those who don't,
slippers the slippers,
muffles how and why
for what
fits between teeth, stopped
throttling laughter long ago, can't
hear last may let alone
baruch ata adonai
or much else but dürer dürer
his name oiled in black,
echo contraptions of paint.

Immigration

At the center of three years
you hear, *Hier ist die Schokolade,*
not as if it was shouted
through floors thought
soundproof, the German
family's first words, chocolate
hidden all this time
the drumming,
sparring, dancing, snoring
they must have endured.
The library is lonely here,
no one to track
you've taken out Kant,
thermodynamics, Java Script.
Another secret that shouldn't be kept:
on Sunday you can recycle,
drop your glass, let it shatter
inside the sidewalk metal bins
at ten-fifteen, ten-thirty, noon,
or nine pm. The church bells
accomplices, camouflage dissent.

Freebooter

If it had only been egg on her face
she still could have walked into a room and smiled
to the center of each sidelong glance,
but what she wore was a deluxe oil slick.
She jumped the cliff, was slapped
across the soles of her feet by the lake's face
streaked with rainbows that traced the contours
of cheekbones, nose, chin, stretched
a second skin, underlined her eyes
and lashes with tarry flecks. There is a shore
in every direction, more than one stroke
to swim there, perimeters of people
with life preservers and megaphones.
They never tire of watching her change
directions. Each rest she sinks, each sink
gathers another piece of the floor and piles.

Performance Review

Her skills were so soft they competed
in the cloud olympics, floated away,
floated a win. The clouds had less
will, more directives from oceans,
mountains, and winds. Her skills
had so much understanding,
couldn't leave her, hovered,
their bulk haloed between
her and what could have been
a blinding beyond.

User Manual

Where you see a salmagundi
of girls, feet barnacle scoured,
salted, and cured, learn
the shape of the shore by balance
atop trees given in to the ground.
In the grain, polished
as tarnished silver, consider the fun
house warp, the sand, too,
catches you in as many
reflections as the sun. The log
you can't possibly drag
into the sound
is the one to sky an oar,
let your legs rudder,
float you past not a prayer.

Portage

The man driving the house
yells in French, a stone wall
infringes, tail lights fracture,
cars gather on either side,
an American couple has lost
all they carried except a packet
of cheese on the back seat
sweating in its paper wraps,
not the work of French
thieves. Window nuggets
on the seats and floor,
frames empty, for now
it's as if they're rolled down.
They'll never be late
to Lyon if they stay,
watch the new *pied-à-terre*
dropped and melded
to coastal loam, daubed
with stretched cloud, rose
water, iron enriched glass.

II.

Even your footprints can't find you.
—Ruth Ellen Kocher, "Pleurisy"

Lost at Last

If you leave your ledge
head a thousand miles
east you'll be in the west
wealth of rivers to batter
and fling you a good
long stretch but you'll ground
before the gulf so
much lapping from banks
along the way peep's
glow on your back
third eye
gone awry in mountains
ranging with if
the puma knows where you are
you can't really be
lost though you fly
a few thousand more
than thousands above the deep
elongated puddle
river its handle
cannot take you
anywhere stare
long enough and silt will make
out and off with your eyes.

Re: Happy Weekend

I hope you have a happy weekend,
too, and that you aren't reading this
today or tomorrow, that the S-days
spill into next week when you
won't be reading this
either you are walking a remote path
to dinosaur tracks seen in stone
through the clear glass of river,
felt with your fast losing feeling
feet or resting near a family
pitching *bastas* and *prestos*
while passing crusty breads draped
with various pinks of slivered meats
they've hooved to the center of Ercolano.
Ruins, the theme of the weekend
I hope you ravage till its bones
form a scaffold from which you watch
your workaday self toil and toss
a bone once in a while to remind
what it takes to find marrow.

Labyrinth

In the novel she's never writing
it's unclear if the heroine
saw a black bear swim the inside
passage or the dim green smear
of aurora borealis, fed a seagull
from her hand, recognized herself
in its scraggly feather cut
and scrappy pluck, molested
or was, wore the same orange suit
or changed into found ill-fitting capris,
played her guitar well or poorly
with the pride that brings shame
to all who brush misshapen
pauses ringed by wrong notes
with even the most frayed and split
stereocilia of embedded snail shells
that carry inward whatever's without.

Entropy

The morning he was up
at three he didn't come back
in one piece. From beside
his warm imprint
she hears a door rasp
across tiles and humph
into its frame.

He's only a few days home
from far east. Perhaps left
others behind. When he returns
to his hole in the bed
he smells like river,
algae and silt, his hair cold.

She holds what she can,
wonders where they'll be by
sun's next sinister wink.

Torch

Two women met for brunch.

While the invited cut her pancakes
into propagating triangular stacks
the inviter folded her up, plaid
flowered into squared off
spirals, hair pleated, argyle
divided and helixed her neck,
expert origami in a sequence of tucks.

As paper she could no longer drink
her bloody mary. Even licking her fingertips
stained oil around her now
yellow chrysanthemum lips, could hardly
muster friction enough to make thanks
and I'd better be going
audible, just whispers of crisp sheets
except for grit in her throat
that scraped some words together.

She was able to pay with ruffles from her skirt
and walked most of the way home before the wind
picked her up, its threads a zipline purr
a blur until it bucks a gust to back and forth
descent into a spinney of birch. In the center of a circle
of oscillating voices varied as the highs and lows
of a shifting avalanche, she aims for the heart,
sculpts the flame in a flash that sparks
the bangs of an ascending mezzo sopranic blaze.

More to Will than that You Will

When your idol asks for ideas
on teaching a book
that binds you by cardio vertices
or [insert fantasy here]
reply you'll think about it
which you will and do
and never share except
maybe here
and don't worry
that the nonpareil is waiting
for your response. The land
on which we go Dutch
now spans satellites.
With each yes
ostensibly endless green
thumbs light up.

Yin Yokes

I.

At sixteen, after school they baked bread,
ate it with jam in the yard, bound
by forest. The house was filled with stone birds,
wood shelves, wool blankets, leather shoes,
a film projector, scenes of a retro modern family.
One told the other how her mother
used to sneak into the yard and smoke.
Sneak, in that it was her secret
before the wild flinging off of clothes
in the philanthropist's pantry, the small space
and falling spices a little like the boats
on which she came of age. Had she smoked
for boredom, home all day, daughters in school,
no reward in keeping house, or was it rebellion,
resentment of days, empty
as sockets, pointed eyes staring at the room
waiting for something to power, or anything
to lure her out the door to the edge
of the woods?

II.

Have you ever leaned out the window,
your body anchored to a high room
by your waist at the thickly painted sill, a man
on a bench five floors down as still
as the tree stretched out above him,
while you take deep breaths
through a soft burning roll
of wrapped tobacco,
careful on each exhale to blow church
or school-ward, empty on an orange-fuzz-on-limestone
late autumn Sunday afternoon?

The website for which you string
and stack code hums with increasing urgency,
a clearing of the throat reminder of what
needs to be done, its glow the only light
in the room, which happens to be a kitchen
where you spend most of your time
not cooking. What if you never broke,
never took deep breaths, whether they're
salty sea breeze or smoke? Let them be
as they are: the yoking of sun and moon.

III.

Though maybe it's best to give up
this most common yoga.
Heat in the lungs when yang is away.
Don't you wonder
if there's something you can
only have without? I always follow
wonder. It takes the most
perplexing routes to the soles of your shoes.

III.

The sky is a hole.
We don't fit in.
—Yannis Ritsos, "December 2"

Side Ways

A country of men will watch you climb
a ladder, some point or fetch a net
to place at the base, some scramble ahead
to bring the wheelhouse to you
in pieces: a chart for navigation that unfolds
wider than your arms can span. Another
offers the view and keeps the wheel
spinning in his own hands. One will gather
straw from the barn loft's hiding place,
hide you just where you are, one light
falling straw mid-air—homemade fireworks,
another will reach for a propeller
with one hand, you with the other and make
you the spiral you've drawn in margins
all these years. If you climb with one hand
on the cool rust of the bars, the other out
they'll take turns touching
calluses earned guiding nets, building
a new shelter each night with mad
hammering up and down the guitar neck.

Apples to Apples, Dust to Dust

Tissue wraps Japanese pears and persimmons
to remind they are rare
as the peach chiffon saris

nuns wear and the priest green-fingered
unwinds. He thinks he's visiting
Eden after Eden but each

is a shadow of Potemkin's Village,
the fruit juiced with worry
for right and wrong, who's next

and who was, all trying to believe
in polyamory. He says shock
is a quake that breaks the ground

shared by beholder
and beheld. His fingers
in the folds, like worms

sup on fronds and flesh, convert
what they can into shrouds
impossible to arrange on living fruit.

Air Craft

To be fair, he was only a part-time priest,
the job description written by God
in a negative space contrail script
only he understood. The rest of us,
not having read his contract, didn't know
when it was down-time or off-time,
didn't see his hands coming.
Fingers crossing his heart
one moment and the next they're crossing
yours. You who find your way to this
dirt packed state where the president's wife's
thumbprint signs her name, hoping
your newly acquired head bobble
would shake the heavy blond mulleted head
from yours. We all know bed is best
for forgetting. Lucky your life has lasted
long enough to shed most of many
part-time lovers' threads. Toss some in the air
next time a jet goes by, study drag and gather.

One-Thousand, One-Hundred, and Ninety-Six Day Drift

When the others gather, clumps
of faces at the computer
windows either side of madness
that goes by Heartland,
she misses you
in her stewed strawberry voice
that pours in rushes of whole
berry sweetness
but when screens dim and fold
she is quiet
reminding how empty
the heart's land can be.

On the Cusp

No generation to own or
two to outrun
falling wreckage of
her sun caught
on the horns of capricorn
moon a charm on the chain
of halley's comet
inklings not quite touching
her tongue toes
at the edge of this
heart could fall
from it any beat but doesn't
know her data's
rooted in the system
veined and arteried
to heel crust, fingerprint.

Test-tube with a View

Here it's so clean
static clings our feet
to ribbons
of possible routes
ants rush along
your voice
also magnetic
bats back
and forth echoes
in the quarry
of my ear I
try to drag
through mud
buff across
sand melt
on sunned car
roofs. I've
always wanted to be your
ant but what
about a seed?
Each unfastening
floats unknown
and unknowing
where it will alight.
This time a weed,
maybe next a color
so infectious you catch.

Shira **Richman's** poems can be found in *Bayou, Copper Nickel, [PANK], Third Coast, Spoon River Poetry Review, Crab Creek Review,* her chapbook, "Eden Was Here," (Dancing Girl Press 2014), and elsewhere. She has published interviews with Dorianne Laux, Lynn Emanuel, Prageeta Sharma, Tess Gallagher, and Fady Joudah in *Willow Springs.* Her interview with Jake Adam York can be found at *The Volta.*

After earning her MFA in creative writing at Eastern Washington University in Spokane, Washington, she moved to Denver, where she taught literature and writing at the Colorado School of Mines.

Currently, she lives in Bavaria, where she designs books for Burnside Review Press and Racing Form Press and works at the adidas global headquarters.

CPSIA information can be obtained
at www.ICGtesting.com
Printed in the USA
LVOW11s1018211216
518216LV00001B/71/P